Maddy's Amazing African Birthday

by Megan K. Williams
photos by Alessandro Vallecchi
and Maddalena Vallecchi Williams

Library and Archives Canada Cataloguing in Publication

Williams, Megan K., 1965-

Maddy's amazing African birthday / by Megan K. Williams.

ISBN 978-1-897187-47-0

1. Tanzania—Juvenile fiction. 2. Tanzania—Juvenile literature. 3. Tanzania—Pictorial works—Juvenile literature. I. Title.

PS8645.I453M33 2009   jC813'.6   C2008-907697-4

Printed in China

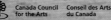

ONTARIO ARTS COUNCIL
CONSEIL DES ARTS DE L'ONTARIO

Canada Council   Conseil des Arts
for the Arts   du Canada

Second Story Press gratefully acknowledges the support of the Ontario Arts Council and the Canada Council for the Arts for our publishing program. We acknowledge the financial support of the Government of Canada through the Book Publishing Industry Development Program.

Published by
Second Story Press
20 Maud Street, Suite 401
Toronto, Ontario, Canada
M5V 2M5
www.secondstorypress.ca

Second Story Press

Maddy's Amazing African Birthday

by Megan K. Williams
photos by Alessandro Vallecchi
and Maddalena Vallecchi Williams

Dad and I were in the kitchen making homemade pasta when the phone rang.

"Maddy, it's for you!" I was covered in flour, but I was too excited to stop and wipe my hands. I almost bumped into my sister who was on her way into the kitchen with the phone. Mom appeared out of nowhere and Dad winked and nodded as I grabbed the receiver. This must be the surprise everyone had been hinting about for days.

"Happy Birthday, Maddy!" my Uncle Alessandro's voice boomed through the receiver.

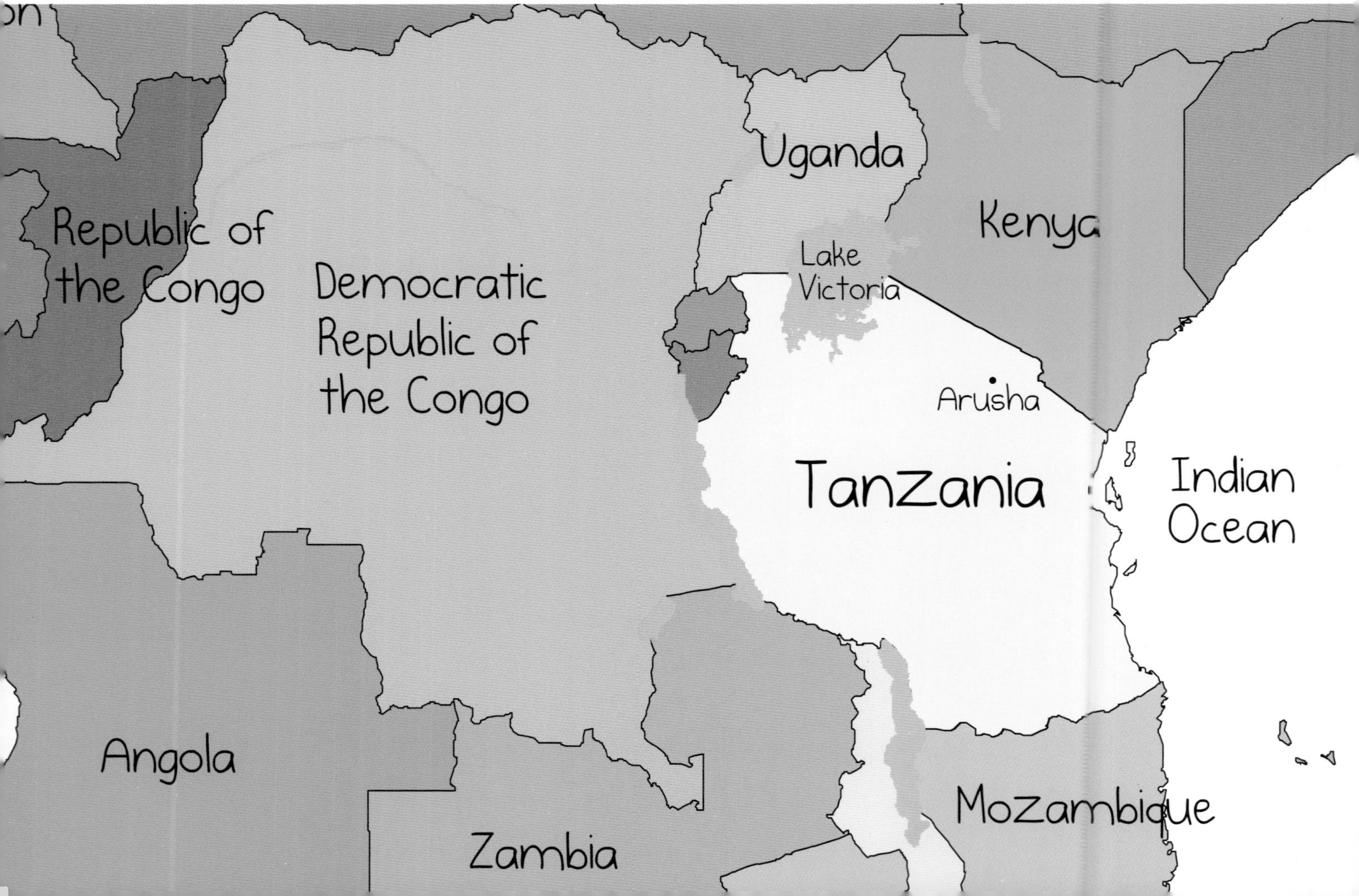

Uganda

Republic of the Congo

Democratic Republic of the Congo

Kenya

Lake Victoria

Arusha

Tanzania

Indian Ocean

Angola

Zambia

Mozambique

Uncle Alessandro is so cool. He travels the world over and tells amazing stories. I have a big map on my wall so I can always check out where he is.

"Maddy," he said, "I'd like you to go to the map in your room."

I rushed to the map. Everyone crowded around me with goofy grins on their faces. My uncle told me to put my finger on Africa and read out the countries, starting at the top. I slid my finger down as I read. "Egypt... Sudan... Uganda... Tanzania..."

"Stop!" said my uncle.

I looked closer at Tanzania. It was a big country on the east coast of the continent. There was the huge Lake Victoria at the top and the Indian Ocean to the right.

"How would you like to travel there to celebrate your birthday?" my uncle asked.

Africa!? I was totally stunned. I'd never even been to a Disney park. Then images of giraffes, zebras, monkeys, and elephants popped into my head. Before I knew it, I was jumping and twirling around the room. Without even meaning to, I let out this ridiculous lion's roar. Everyone laughed, but I didn't care.

I was going to Africa!

One long month later, I sat with my face squashed up against the plane window. It had been hard to wait, but there had been lots of things to buy and pack before I was ready. I was dying to go on a real African safari. Lately I'd hardly been able to sleep just thinking about the trip. I was also a little nervous. I didn't really know what to expect. I was going to be so far away from my family and friends.

Down below, long squiggles of muddy rivers ran like snakes across the brown earth. Uncle Alessandro tapped my shoulder and pointed up ahead. Rooftops glinted in the sun.

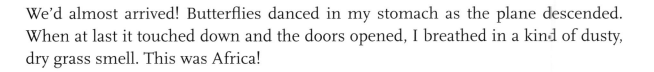

"There's Arusha," he said.

We'd almost arrived! Butterflies danced in my stomach as the plane descended. When at last it touched down and the doors opened, I breathed in a kind of dusty, dry grass smell. This was Africa!

A tall man with a friendly smile was waiting for us at the airport. He was our guide, Nimrod.

"Mambo," he said, in a deep voice. That meant "How's it going?" Dad had helped me learn a few Swahili words before I left.

"Pao!" I answered, which meant "Everything's cool."

Nimrod seemed surprised. "I see you speak Swahili already."

"Not really," I said. I figured I'd better admit those were just about the only words I knew before Nimrod decided to have a whole conversation in Swahili!

Speaking Swahili

When I was in Tanzania, I learned a bunch of Swahili words that came in handy. (I love the way Swahili sounds: it rhymes with "pop a wheelie.") Here are a few words you can use if you ever meet someone from Tanzania – or if you just want to impress your friends!

Wewe Unaitwaje?
What's your name?

Jina langu ni ...
My name is ...

Saa ngapi?
What time is it?

Habari?
How are you?

Nina njaa sana!
I am very hungry!

Tafadhali / Asante
Please / Thank you.

Ndio / Hapana.
Yes / No

Kwaheri!
Good-bye!

Pencils in Arusha

Before we headed out to the Serengeti, we stopped at the Arusha market. It was way more crowded than any mall I'd ever been to. Bananas, hairy coconuts, and shiny melons sat in stacks in tiny, crowded stalls. Uncle Alessandro found a stall that sold boxes of pencils and bought some. He said a lot of the schools in the area we'd be visiting don't have a lot of money. So giving out things like pencils is a small way to help them out while you visit their community.

Once we were in the car and on the road, I realized how different everything was from home. We drove past streams of people on foot. Most of the children wore school uniforms and the women were wrapped in brightly colored, patterned cloth. I was amazed at the gigantic baskets of fruit and sky-high stacks of bread they could carry on their heads – no hands! Uncle Alessandro said it was the best way to carry heavy loads.

Out of the city, even the roads were a different color – a bright, rusty dust lifted up and swirled in the air as cars passed.

I was tired from all the traveling and excitement and had to struggle to stay awake. Finally, we reached the Serengeti. It's the vast plain that in Swahili means "the land that goes on forever."

As the sun was setting, we finally reached the first game park, where we would be staying. Since it was full of wild animals, I was pretty relieved to see the campsite. Two welcoming chairs sat outside the tent, and inside were two of the most comfy-looking beds I had ever seen. There was even a clean, wooden floor!

Before we went to bed, we sat around a campfire. I listened to the crackling flames and strange night sounds and followed the sparks upward with my eyes. The African night sky was bursting with a trillion stars! I felt so lucky to be on this adventure.

When I opened my eyes the next morning, I was surrounded by drapes of white gauze. Where the heck was I? Then I heard a long screech and remembered. Right! Under a mosquito net! The screech was from an obnoxious monkey that had carried on half the night somewhere near the tent.

I remembered something else too, and got up and dressed in a hurry. Today we were going on a safari. That's another Swahili word, meaning "trip."

We left as the sun was making orange-pink streaks across the sky. We had to get a move on if we wanted to see any wildlife, because it would be boiling hot by noon and time for the animals to sleep.

Nimrod opened the Jeep roof so I could stand up and be on the lookout for lions and elephants. I was glad Mom and Dad weren't around to make me buckle up! I loved the feeling of wind whipping through my hair and all the space around me. Freedom!

Marvelous Mounds

I'd seen big anthills before, but I'd never seen ones taller than me! Termite mounds aren't really anthills, though. They're the nests of bugs called termites, which look like big, white ants, even if they're not even related to ants.

Termites eat rotten trees and plants and that makes them really important to the environment. They are major recyclers – munching old wood and pooping out fertile dirt.

The mounds are all over the Serengeti and they are home to thousands – sometimes millions – of termites. But it's not just termites that use the mounds. Cheetahs sometimes sit on top of them to look for animals to hunt!

On and on we drove, for what seemed like forever. The sun rose higher in the sky. Still, I hardly saw any animals; just a few antelopes in the distance. Maybe it was dumb, but I was expecting it to be like the movies, with herds of zebras and giraffes all over the place. Instead, there were wide, empty plains. What was I going to tell my friends back home? That I'd seen some awesome grass and termite mounds?

When we stopped to have some sandwiches, I lost my cool and blurted, "I could have stayed at home and seen more animals on TV!" I wish I hadn't, especially when I saw the look on my uncle's face. He was hurt – and annoyed. He told me that camera crews spend weeks waiting around to get those great shots on film. "Learn to be patient," he kept saying.

Patient! I hated that word.

After lunch, Nimrod steered the Jeep toward a river, where he said we might see some animals coming for their end-of-the-day drink. On the way, the Jeep braked sharply. Nimrod handed me the binoculars and pointed at a nearby tree. Huge hot-dog things dangled from it. Weird. Nimrod said it was a *kigelia* or sausage tree.

"Look closer," he said.

Climbing Cats

Leopards used to live all over the world, but now they are mostly just in Africa. That's because people took up more and more of the land, and leopards couldn't survive in the places that were left.

You can tell a leopard by its spots, which look sort of like little black roses. These cats are super fast. They can run up to 37 miles an hour (60 kilometers) — not quite as fast as my dad likes to drive, but almost! They are also great climbers and love to laze about high up on branches. Leopards aren't as big as lions, but they've got really big heads. That means they can open their jaws wide to eat everything they catch. Look out antelopes!

I moved the binoculars around and saw something else that was dangling; something that flickered. I followed it upwards. A leopard's tail! The huge cat it belonged to was stretched lazily along a branch.

My uncle couldn't believe it. He grabbed the binoculars from me and stared. Then he shook his head. "Do you know how many times I've been to Africa and never seen a leopard?"

"Guess you had to be more patient!" I said.

We all burst out laughing. I suddenly felt much better about the day, and not just because I'd seen a leopard.

We drove along the riverbank, and guess what we saw there? A whole family of elephants – including a baby. Nimrod told me that park rangers try hard to protect the elephants from poachers. Poachers are people who hunt elephants for their ivory tusks, which they sell, even though it's against the law. Trade in ivory is illegal, but poachers don't care. I watched as the baby kept slipping in the mud and its mother kept hauling it back up with her trunk. I couldn't imagine how anyone could hurt them. I wish we could have stayed and watched them forever, but it was getting late so we had to leave. As we drove away, I closed my eyes and made a wish: that the baby elephant would grow up strong and free.

Some Baby!

I found out that African elephants are the largest land animals on Earth. They're bigger than the ones in India – even their ears are bigger. Look at a picture of an African elephant's ear and then look at a map of Africa. Notice any similarities?

Nimrod told me that the males, called bulls, live on their own. Females are called cows and they live in a herd of mothers and babies. Mothers stay pregnant for almost two whole years before they give birth – more than twice as long as humans. The babies weigh 200 pounds (91 kg) when they are born. The adults eat up to 300 pounds (136 kg) of grass, fruit, and roots a day! Good thing they do a lot of walking.

Every day we saw little villages with their small houses and herds of bony goats and cows. Kids chased after the Jeep as we sped past.

"Jambo!" – "Hey there!" they called. Uncle Alessandro always waved back. At first I was shy. I mean, it was only us – we weren't exactly movie stars. Then I started waving too, and it was kind of fun.

But today was different. We were actually visiting a Maasai village. The Maasai are nomads. They don't stay in the same place for long, though they do stay long enough to build little houses. Guess what they are made of? Sticks and cow poop But they don't smell at all and when you touch the walls, they're almost as hard as the walls at home.

When we arrived, a bunch of moms and little kids came up to greet us. The women were very tall and thin and wore tons of beaded jewelry. They had huge holes in their ears for earrings. I asked Nimrod if they were painful and he told me the holes are made when children are young and they are taught to be brave. Still, it must have hurt a bit.

Maasai Jewelry

Red is the favorite color for Maasai clothing. But when it comes to their beaded jewelry, they like pretty much every color. Blue, green, white, and orange, too. Blue represents the sky and green stands for grass, which is really important for their cows. Even red and blue are about cattle. Red stands for the cow's blood and white stands for milk.

The women make the jewelry. They are also the ones who get to wear it. The best thing is, Maasai women don't wear their beadwork just on special occasions, but all the time! The older and more important you are, the more jewelry you get to wear.

Everyone wanted to feel my hair! The kids had never touched long, straight hair before and they were super curious. I had friends at home with hair like theirs, but to them, my hair was different from anything they'd seen.

The kids were really cute, but a lot of them had runny noses with flies buzzing all around their faces. One little girl had an awful cough. I remembered the emergency pack that Mom and I had put together for the trip. It was in the back of the Jeep, and in it was a big bottle of cough syrup. Uncle Alessandro had been giving out boxes of pencils to the school children we passed, but I'd been too shy. Here was my chance. I asked him if it would be okay to give the cough syrup to the little girl.

"What if you get sick and need it?" he asked.

"I won't!" I said. Besides, I thought, if I did need it, we could afford to buy some more. These kids couldn't.

"Well, it's your decision," my uncle said.

I ran to the Jeep and got the medicine. Nimrod translated as I handed the bottle to the mother and explained how many spoonfuls to give each day. She was really pleased and squeezed my hand to say thanks. It was just a little thing, but it felt good.

I hated to leave the village, but Nimrod said we had one more stop to make that day. It was at a lake called Natron that was full of bright, pink flamingos. When we got there, I couldn't believe how many there were! Thousands upon thousands of birds crowded in the lake. Alessandro told me they were eating the bacteria in the shallow water.

Pink Alert!

Flamingos love living in big groups, which explains what thousands of them were doing together in Lake Natron the day I was there. They stand around in shallow mud all day eating shrimp (that's what makes them so pink) and bacteria. Germs to us, food to them!

Even though there were more flamingos than I could count, they could all die soon. People have a plan to pump water out of the lake so they can get the ash from the mud. They want to sell the ash to factories because it is used to make soap. But with less ash in the lake, the bacteria could die. And the flamingos need the bacteria to stay alive. If the plan goes through, the flamingos are in big danger.

We met some Maasai men on the shore of the lake. They were looking for a lost cow. Cattle are worth a lot of money to the Maasai. Losing a cow there would be kind of like losing a car back home. We promised we would keep an eye out for it, but before they went on their way, we asked if we could take their picture. The men formed a circle and took turns seeing who could jump the highest. They were amazing! Uncle Alessandro joined in and fell flat on his bum! I laughed so hard my stomach ached.

Traveling isn't always fun. Take, for instance, the day our Jeep got stuck.

All morning long, Nimrod had driven in zigzags, trying to avoid potholes. Then we ended up getting stuck in a patch of soft sand! The wheels spun around and around, shooting sand up in the air like a fountain.

We all had to get out of the Jeep and collect rocks to put under the tires so they could grip better, but nothing worked. My uncle was really grumpy. He kicked the tire and swore. It was super tense. Finally, Nimrod said he would run ahead to the next village and bring help.

Waiting was hot and boring until a woman came along the road selling shiny, bronze bracelets. She didn't speak English, but when Uncle Alessandro asked, "How much?" she held up ten fingers. She wanted ten shillings, which is what they call money in Tanzania. My uncle shook his head and held up five fingers. Then the woman held up nine fingers and my uncle held up six. Then she held up eight and he held up seven. Finally, she shook her head. Eight was the lowest she would go.

By now, Uncle Alessandro was smiling and laughing. He seemed to have forgotten all about being stuck in the sand. When the bargaining was done and I had slipped on my new bracelet, Nimrod was back with some helpers.

They pushed the Jeep out and we all piled in and drove to the village. There, a woman invited us into her house and showed us how she made flour. With a rough, heavy stone, she ground up something called cassava root, which is kind of like a potato. The flour reminded me of making pasta with Dad, except for the odd bug that landed in the cassava flour.

African Nomads

All nomads move around, but they don't all live the same way. The Hadzapi people hunt for a living. But they also collect roots, wild fruit, and honey. In fact, the way they survive hasn't changed much for thousands of years. Other nomads, like the Maasai, live off the meat and milk of animals – cows, goats, or sheep. It's tough being a nomad these days, though. Because of global warming, there have been more droughts. This makes it harder to find vegetation to feed the animals. More and more nomads now are giving up on their wandering ways.

A day I'll never ever forget was when we visited the Hadzapi tribe. The Hadzapi are nomads too, except unlike the Maasai, they don't build houses, or even tents. Instead, they sleep beside a campfire to keep warm and safe from animals.

The Hadzapi are famous for their incredible hunting skills. When we arrived, some boys were practicing shooting arrows at a log. Not one of them missed! The boys showed me how they put poison on the metal

arrow tip so the animals die more quickly and don't suffer. They'd already killed a monkey that day. Its insides were drying on a tree and they asked me if I'd wanted to try some. No thanks!

It was my turn to try the bow and arrow. The bow was way heavier than it looked and it was hard to hold up and keep steady. I pulled the arrow back as far as I could, but it plopped to the ground right in front of me. Everyone laughed like it was the most hilarious thing they had ever seen. I felt so clutzy! Then Uncle Alessandro tried. He did better because he's bigger, but he didn't get the arrow anywhere near the log. At least I wasn't the only one!

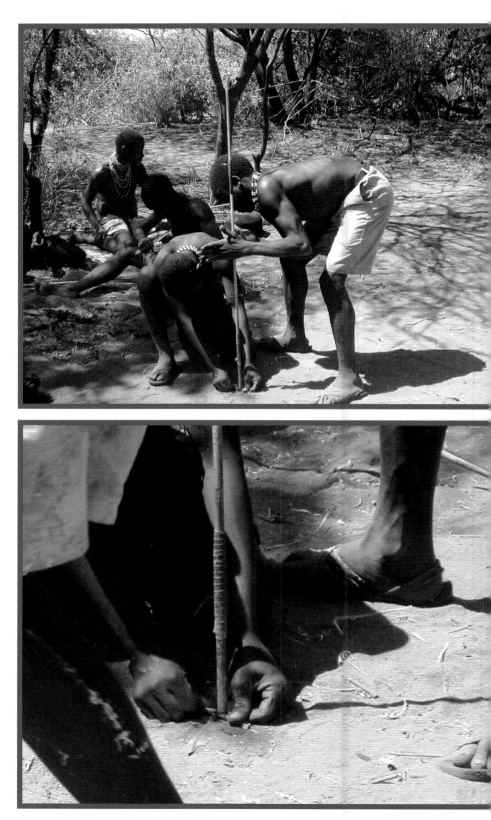

The kids showed me how they make a fire. They took a long stick and rolled it back and forth against a block of wood on the ground. A wisp of smoke swirled, and pretty soon, up leapt a little flame. The boys added dry leaves and little sticks and soon they had a real fire going.

After that, we all got in a circle and sang and danced together. The kids made cool clicking sounds with their tongues when they sang. I tried to teach them Ring Around the Rosy, but it didn't go that well, except for the "all-fall-down" part, which cracked everybody up.

Before we left, the kids showed me how they make quill necklaces. Now that I knew how to bargain, I bought a whole bunch. Guess what all my friends got as gifts?

On our last day, Nimrod invited us to his house to meet his family. He lived in a house pretty much like houses back home. It had electricity and a bathroom and a television.

Nimrod had two children. They had the neatest names – Azizi and Bakari. In English, they meant Precious and Promise. We had delicious guava juice inside and then went out and played soccer, just like at home. But the best thing was – they spoke my language! Finally I could talk with other kids!

Soon, Nimrod would be taking us to the airport and we would be flying back home. I was sad to be leaving Africa, but I really wanted to go home, too. I had so much to tell everyone about: the animals I'd seen, the different way people lived, playing with the Hadzapi kids, and now Azizi and Bakari....

It was funny, because I'd only been away two weeks but I felt really different. Like I was both bigger and smaller. Bigger, because I had done a lot of new stuff, and smaller, because I now realized I was just a tiny part of a very big world. The strange thing was, it didn't make me feel bad. It was the opposite. It made me feel light and free... like jumping for joy.

I flung myself into a crazy twirl. Azizi and Bakari laughed.

I couldn't wait to see more of the world one day.